Arctic Birds
For Kids

Amazing Animal Books
For Young Readers

By
Rachel Smith

Mendon Cottage Books
JD-Biz Corp Publishing

Read More Amazing Animal Books

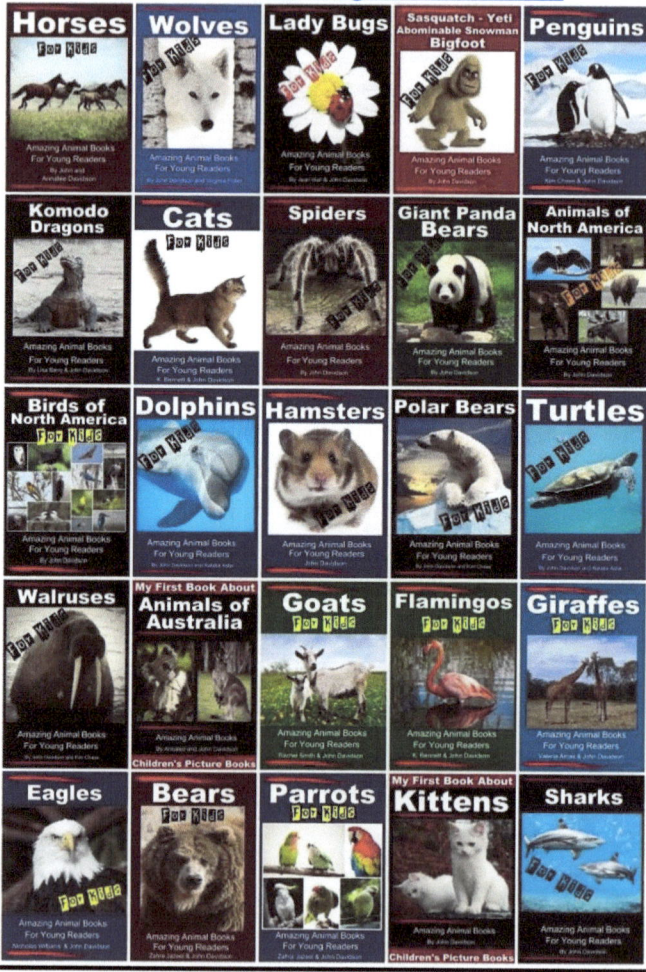

Purchase at Amazon.com

Table of Contents

Introduction 4

What is an Arctic bird?..5

What is the Arctic like? 7

The history of Arctic birds and humans......................................10

Puffins 12

Snow geese..15

Arctic terns 17

Tundra swans 19

Auklets 21

Snowy owls..23

Grey herons...25

Conclusion 27

Author Bio 28

Publisher 29

Introduction

One thing many people can't say they've seen in their Arctic habitat is an Arctic bird. Most Arctic birds don't stay permanently in the Arctic, and tend to travel south for the warmth. However, despite many of the folks in the upper areas of the northern hemisphere (upper half of the world) seeing them during the winter, it's still a rare person who knows and understands how Arctic birds act and live in their Arctic setting.

The typical Arctic bird is not really beautiful. Majestic, maybe, in the cases of eagle and even owls. Perhaps even powerful or scary.
However, for most Arctic birds, there is a distinct lack of pretty colors and brilliant plumage. The puffin is a bit of an exception, with its bright beak and other attention-grabbing features, but even it loses them when it goes north.

If you've ever wondered where these birds go in the summer, or are just curious about Arctic birds, sit back. You are about to be enlightened.

What is an Arctic bird?

An Arctic bird, to be plain, is a bird that lives, at least part of the time, in the Arctic. This isn't to be confused with Antarctic birds such as penguins. Antarctica is on the opposite end of the globe, and you won't find penguins in the Arctic.

Atlantic puffins, a kind of Arctic bird.

These are birds that have evolved to live in the cold. Unlike penguins in the south, they leave their Arctic home every year, often for mating and migrating. Arctic winters are not kind, and even these birds find themselves looking for somewhere to spend the winter.

Many of these birds are black, black and white, or mostly white. This makes sense because they live in snow, and white is going to give them an advantage. The birds that live primarily in Arctic oceans tend to be darker; the birds that live on the land tend to be lighter.

Most of these birds are hunters. Some hunt fish, others hunt other birds and small mammals. This is because there is only so much food available in the Arctic, as it is generally a harsh environment.

There are many, many types of Arctic birds that we can't cover in this book; the ones mentioned are some the major ones, or better known ones. Puffins, for instance, are very well known throughout the world, though some people mistake them for penguins of some kind due to their coloring.

Grey herons and snowy owls are also very well known in North America, for the most part. Folks more to the South may not know them, but in areas such as Canada and the northern part of the United States of America, many know them. The snowy owl is also well known in Eurasia (which is Europe and Asia), as it lives there too.

What is the Arctic like?

The Arctic is less of a land mass like Antarctica and more like a general area. It is not a continent, which is a very large mass of land, as much of it is made up of oceans and ice. It is situated at the North Pole. The Earth has two poles: the South Pole, and the North. This are magnetic centers, and they influence how the Earth works.

The Arctic during the summer.

The area around the North Pole is called a polar region (much like polar bears, which live in that area). It is filled with glaciers and permafrost. Much of the Arctic boundaries are not specific, though. Scientifically, the line is where the trees stop. There are no trees in the scientific

Arctic. However, for the countries that line the edges, they consider their states Arctic.

This includes a part of these places: Alaska (a state in America, much further to the North), Finland, Norway, Iceland, Sweden, Russia, and then Greenland, which is a nation that is sort of owned by Denmark.

The Arctic during the winter. This in particular is Svalbard, an island owned by Norway and settled by very few people.

Many peoples have lived in the Arctic, as have many kinds of animals, especially fish, birds, and various predators, such as the polar bear. However, a lot of the area considered Arctic by these countries is actually called subarctic. This means it's below the scientific Arctic.

However, these places get very cold too, and have a lot of the effects of the Arctic.

For one thing, due to the Earth's rotation, the Arctic has an unusual night and day pattern going on. For most of the year, it is quite dark in the Arctic. However, when its short summer comes, light is about day-long, so there is pretty much no night. This is when the plants do their growing. They make up an area called tundra, which means there is frozen ground but things still grow on it in the summer. In the winter, the plants are covered with snow.

Despite its reputation, the Arctic only gets about twenty inches of snow on average. It seems like it's snowing more often than it is because of wind; it's fairly dry in the Arctic, so the snow is easily whipped up and blown about.

There are also a lot of glaciers and sea ice in the Arctic. However, this amount has been going down for at least the past three decades, if not much more. The area considered Arctic has also been getting smaller for the same amount of time, especially in the past three decades. Some estimates put it at about 105 miles of Arctic lost.

The seas (there are about a dozen considered Arctic) are also cold. To be clear, even the land doesn't get warm; winters are extremely cold, and summers are only cool. The animals that live in the seas tend to be well equipped for keeping body heat in, and also eat a lot of food to produce the heat they need.

The history of Arctic birds and humans

Humans have long been interested in Arctic birds and have used them. The ones that are in North America have long been hunting targets for the native peoples, such as the Inuit, and other birds that dwell in Europe and Asia have long been used for food.

A pair of parakeet auklets. This type of bird has not had much trouble with humans.

For instance, puffins are a huge source of food in Iceland and the Faroe Islands. They also used to be a huge food source in other areas, such as Greenland, but the hunting of them has been mostly banned throughout the world except in these two areas.

Much of human interaction has been scientific. For example, Linnaeus, in his book of animals quite a few years ago, sketched the snowy owl and put it in his book. Many North American animals made it into this book, though that also has to do with a lot of them also living in Eurasia.

Scientists nowadays are trying to understand and preserve Arctic birds. Birds have been protected from being hunted, for example, and they have been the subject of studies.

Many things are still unknown about many of the birds, however. For instance, seabirds that live on the ocean alone have been very hard to track; little is known about their life at sea, and this is something that sometimes bothers scientists.

There is still so much we don't know about animals, in particular Arctic animals. This is because the climate is so harsh that it's much harder to stay there a while and observe these animals. Also, birds that live on the ocean are very hard to spot, because they blend in with the water and they're often far apart. It's like trying to find a single button in an ocean of buttons.

Puffins

Puffins are one of the best known Arctic birds. There are three recognized kinds: the tufted puffin and the horned puffin, which live in the Pacific side, and the Atlantic puffin, which, unsurprisingly, lives in the Atlantic side.

A tufted puffin.

Puffins share several things in common. For one thing, they eat fish and occasionally other animals. Chiefly, though, it's fish. Puffins can carry more than one fish at a time because of the way their beak moves;

instead of simply opening and closing like other birds' beaks, it can move sideways too.

The most we know about puffins is in their nesting and mating periods. This is because, while puffins come together in these instances, when they are at sea, where they live for all of winter and a bit longer, they are alone. It's pretty much impossible to find a single puffin at sea.

The bright beaks and things like tufts and bright feathers all come off after mating season is over. The puffin only has these bright colors to attract mates. When the colorful overbeak falls off, a smaller, dull beak is there, so it isn't left beak-less.

When puffins come to land to mate and nest, they tend to choose areas for nests such as craggy holes in the cliffs, or burrows left behind by other animals. They like secure places, usually on deserted islands or other hard to reach places. Massive amounts of puffins often go to these areas, to the tune of tens of thousands.

Puffins have one chick at a time. Both parents are devoted to the chick, bringing it food and protecting it. When the chick is ready to fly, it sneaks out during the night so that predators won't eat it, and then goes out to sea for a few years. It finally comes back when it's matured enough to have its own chick, and the mating age is not just a one time thing. This is good, because if every puffin only produced half a chick, there would be no more puffins very quickly.

In fact, puffins have very large populations and are in no danger of dying out any time soon. This is not how it has always been; the Atlantic at least was in very great danger during the 19th century, when it was hunted in huge numbers.

It could have had a fate similar to the passenger pigeon, a bird that was entirely made extinct in the United States and elsewhere in North America in the 20th century due to merciless hunting by a large number of people.

But fortunately, people realized that they did not want this bird to disappear, and they worked together to save it. There are only two places in the world that still hunt puffins, as named, the Faroe Islands, which belong to Denmark, and Iceland, which used to belong to Denmark. Both places rely a lot on things such as fishing and don't have the same farm land opportunities that other countries have, so they need to hunt puffins to sustain themselves.

Snow geese

Snow geese are a conundrum to the scientific community. They can't quite classify them, or at least, they can't agree on it. Some say it's a gray goose family member; others a white goose family member. One thing is for sure, though: these geese go the furthest north out of any type of goose.

Snow geese migrating.

The snow goose is also known as the blue goose. This is because it has what are called morphs. There are two: the white goose morph means the snow goose is white everywhere but its black-blue wingtips. The blue goose morph means that it is brown-blue everywhere but its head. Both types are snow geese, and they interbreed.

There are also two subspecies of the snow goose. One is the lesser snow goose, which is smaller and lives in some parts of Canada and places like Siberia, and then the greater snow goose, which lives in another part of Canada. It is bigger.

The snow goose breeds in the Arctic. Pairs start when they are about two years old, but they don't breed until they are least three. Snow geese tend to mate for life, or at least for the long term. Females lay three to five eggs in a nest lined with their down (soft feathers), and then incubate them for twenty to twenty five days.

The babies leave the nest within hours, and feed themselves. However, the parents look out for them, and the babies stay with their parents until they are two or three years old and go off to find their own mates.

There are millions of this kind of goose.

Arctic terns

The Arctic tern is always in summer. This is the bird that has the longest migration route of any animal in the world by far. The Arctic tern migrates from the Northern summer in the Arctic to the Southern summer in Antarctica. This can be anywhere from 40,000-50,000 miles in a year.

A pair of Arctic terns.

Arctic terns are seabirds. This means that they get their food from the sea. They eat fish and small animals such as crayfish. They also spend a lot of their time at sea. The way they eat is through diving at the water and getting fish.

One interesting thing about them is that they can sometimes take another bird's food. They will swoop at the bird and get them to drop their fish in surprise, and then they take the fish. This is common with other terns, puffins, and other birds.

The Arctic tern was once called the sea swallow, because they are so much like swallows when they fly and dive down to pluck a fish out of the water.

Arctic terns mate for life. Mating is done through a series of flying feats on the part of both male and female, and then the male feeds the female. When she is nesting, he also feeds her, and both work together to protect the nest. This is important, because they are vulnerable to animals, especially cats.

It is a very aggressive bird, and has been known to attack large predators and humans. It can't really damage a human, but it can draw blood.

Tundra swans

Tundra swans are considered to come in two subspecies. Some people think they're separate species entirely, but the scientific community hasn't decided yet. There's the whistler swan, and then there's the Bewick swan.

A tundra swan, surrounded by mallard ducks.

The main difference between the two subspecies is the coloring of the beak. Whistler swans have almost completely black beaks. Bewick swans have a large portion of it that's yellow.

Both kinds are completely white when they're adults; young swans might be more of a gray instead. They also have black feet, and are considered one of the smaller types of Arctic swans.

Tundra swans breed in Arctic or subarctic conditions. After that, they migrate to grasslands and other such places, and often feed on discarded grain. They can fly very high, as high as eight kilometers in the air.

They eat aquatic plants during the summer, and during the winter they tend to eat leftover things from human crops, such as potatoes and grain.

Very few animals hunt the tundra swan. Arctic foxes sometimes try to prey on chicks and nesting females, but tundra swans are very aggressive when nesting and usually scare away the fox.

They are usually pretty friendly when not nesting, though. Not friendly enough to try to keep as a pet, of course, but not likely to attack humans.

There are well over one hundred thousand of them in the world.

Auklets

Auklets are a kind of auk. Auks are the overall group that various birds that live on the ocean belong to, including puffins. Most of them are black and white. They also only come onshore to breed, and otherwise spend their lives at sea.

The crested auklet.

Auklets are a specific group of auks, mostly the smallest ones. The least auklet, the smallest, is only 85 grams and fifteen centimeters.

Like puffins, they eat fish and the occasional invertebrate (which are creatures that don't have spines; humans are vertebrates). Krill, for example, a tiny little thing that blue whales eat, is a common food source for auklets.

An example of a typical enough auklet is the parakeet auklet. It has a small white plume on its head, and blue eyes. It also has an upturned beak, which gives a sort of interesting expression on its face. However, this type of bird does not really have expressions like humans; it's only a thing we think of when we look at it.

It's only twenty-three centimeters. Parakeet auklets are incredibly social when they are breeding colonies, and quite enjoy each other's company. They live alone at sea, and their feathers and such are not very different between breeding and living at sea, unlike the puffin.

Like with most auklets, there are plenty of parakeet auklets: one million, and they aren't considered threatened at all. This is because humans have yet to really intrude upon the Arctic area.

Snowy owls

Snowy owls are some of the more well known Arctic birds. These birds are white, though they tend to have some black on them, the females more than the males. Their babies, however, are born completely white.

A snowy owl in flight.

This type of owl lives in both North America and Eurasia. It's native to the Arctic, and some type of it is said to have once lived in Central Europe (such as Poland) way back in an Ice Age. An Ice Age is when things got much colder on Earth; the last one was a long time ago.

The snowy owl has about three to eleven eggs in a breeding. These are laid every other day until they are done, so none of the babies are quite the same age.

They hatch at different times about five weeks later. In some kinds of birds, a difference in size would mean the babies would kill each other to try to get more food. This isn't the case with snowy owlets, and they tend not to fight with each other at all. The parents make certain all of them get enough food, so there's no reason to fight.

The parents also fight anything that threatens their young. The male stands guard as the female either sits on the eggs or keeps the young warm, but both will attack dogs, arctic foxes, and the like to keep the chicks from being eaten.

Snowy owls hunt mostly lemmings (a kind of rodent) and other small rodents when the breeding season is on. In less kind settings, they tend to go for young ptarmigans (a kind of bird) and other animals.

They often swallow their prey whole if they're small enough. A mouse, for example, would easily be swallowed whole. The snowy owl then kind of spits up the bones and other parts that they can't digest.

Grey herons

The grey heron is not to be confused with its closely related relative, the great blue heron. The great blue heron is not an Arctic bird, while the grey heron often lives as far north as the Arctic circle, which is the area where the true Arctic starts.

Some grey herons.

Grey herons hunt by standing shallow water and grabbing things. These often include frogs, fish, and insects, but they will sometimes eat other birds and reptiles too.

The grey heron is spread very far; it can live as far south as Madagascar, depending on which subspecies it is, and is spread all over Asia, Africa, and Europe during the cooler seasons.

Grey herons in Europe have adapted very well to the urban environment. In Amsterdam, in the Netherlands, the grey heron walks the street and lives in little parks and nesting areas. They even take advantage of humans that will feed them, and will try to get a fisherman to give them part of their catch, which they often do.

They have also been observed moving into zoo exhibits for water creatures such as penguins or seals. They make themselves right at home and eat the food left out for the animals in the exhibit.

Grey herons are not nearly as present in the Arctic as many of the other birds mentioned in this book, but they still are Arctic birds.

Conclusion

Arctic birds come in many shapes and sizes. They also are pretty well protected against human dangers. Very few are endangered in any way.

Still, we have to work to keep things this way. As humans spread their influence, and as the climate changes, we may have to look for ways to serve our Arctic friends.

Hopefully, they will never truly experience the troubles many endangered birds have faced.

Author Bio

Rachel Smith is a young author who enjoys animals. Once, she had a rabbit which was very nervous, and chewed through her leash and tried to escape. She's also had several pet mice, which were the funniest little animals to watch. She lives in Ohio with her family and writes in her spare time.

Publisher

JD-Biz Corp

P O Box 374

Mendon, Utah 84325

http://www.jd-biz.com/

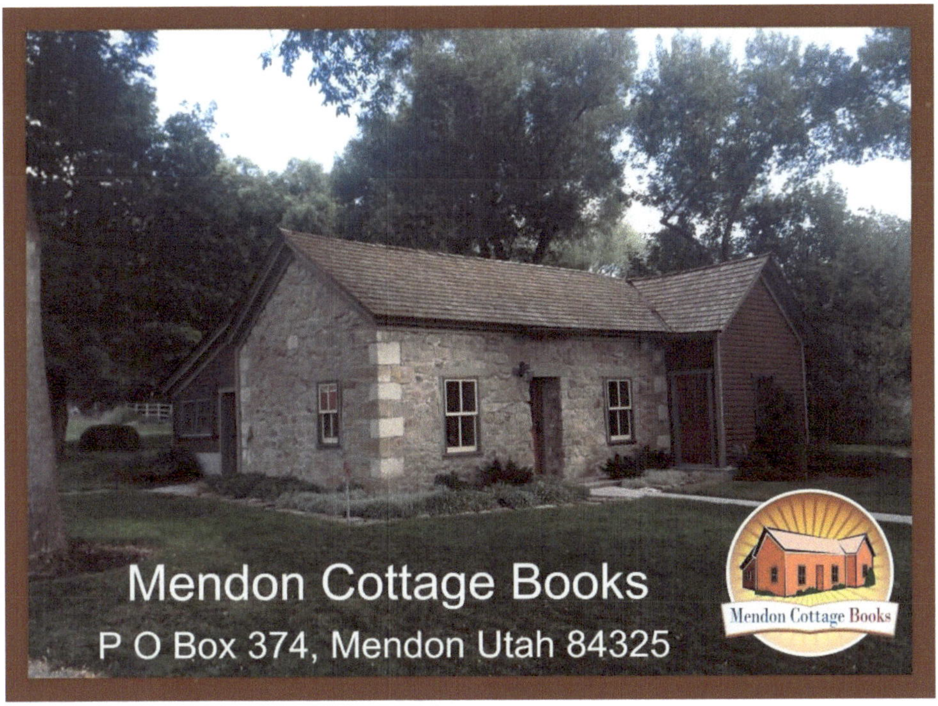

Mendon Cottage Books

P O Box 374, Mendon Utah 84325

Top Ten Dog Breeds For Kids
Amazing Animal Books For Young Readers
Kisha Bennett & John Davidson

German Shepherds
Dog Books for Kids
K. Bennett

Bulldogs
Dog Books for Kids
K. Bennett

Dachshund
Dog Books for Kids
K. Bennett

Poodles
Dog Books for Kids
K. Bennett

Labrador Retrievers
Dog Books for Kids
K. Bennett

Rottweilers
Dog Books for Kids
K. Bennett

Boxers
Dog Books for Kids
K. Bennett

Golden Retrievers
Dog Books for Kids
K. Bennett

Puppies
Dog Books For Kids
Amazing Animal Books
By John Davidson

Beagles
Dog Books for Kids
K. Bennett

Yorkshire Terriers
Dog Books for Kids
K. Bennett

Dogs
Top Ten Dog Breeds For Kids
Amazing Animal Books For Young Readers
Zahra Jazeel & John Davidson

Cats For Kids
Amazing Animal Books For Young Readers
K. Bennett & John Davidson

Foxes For Kids
Amazing Animal Books For Young Readers
Zahra Jazeel & John Davidson

Wolves For Kids
Amazing Animal Books For Young Readers
By John Davidson and Virginia Fidler

www.ingramcontent.com/pod-product-compliance
Lightning Source LLC
Chambersburg PA
CBHW050905290526
45792CB00002B/719